FLOWERS AROUND THE WORLD COLORING BOOK

JANET HAWKINS

RAINBOW LADA PRESS
FLORIDA, USA

Copyright © 2023 by Janet Hawkins

All rights reserved.

You may not distribute any **uncolored** pages in any form including posting on social media, uploading to any website, or through any other method. You may post colored pages on social media sites.

You may scan and print the images for personal use so that you can color them multiple times or print them on a different type of paper.

You may not sell any images from this book, either colored or uncolored without written permission from Rainbow Lada Press.

Published by Rainbow Lada Press
An imprint of Rainbow Lada LLC
2462 Laurel Rd E #573
Nokomis, FL 34275 USA
Email: rainbowlada0@gmail.com

First edition: April 2023
ISBN: 979-8-89035-005-3

This book belongs to

Scientific name of flower

- National flower of COUNTRY
- Interesting fact about the flower

Use this page to test colors and check for bleeding.

Tip: if using markers try putting a blank piece of paper or a piece of plastic underneath each page before coloring.

Note: this page is repeated in the back of the book.

Helianthus annuus

- National flower of Ukraine
- Sunflowers were planted at Chernobyl to help clean nuclear waste.

Sunflower

Plumeria (alba or rubra)

- National flower of Laos
- Also known as frangipani or dok champa, this flower plays a role in the religious Baci ceremony, which is used to welcome guests.

Plumeria

Lilium candidum

- National flower of Italy
- The Madonna lily is a symbol for the Virgin Mary in Catholicism. These flowers have been cultivated for over 3000 years.

Convallaria majalis

- National flower of Finland
- This flower contains poisonous compounds that affect the heart. Historically these flowers were used to make sneezing powder.

Cassia fistula

- National flower of Thailand
- The ratchaphruek, also known as the golden shower tree, is a royal flower and is associated with Buddhism because of its yellow color.

Dahlia pinnata

- National flower of Mexico
- An Aztec name for dahlia was cocoxochitl, meaning water pipe, because they used the hollow stems to transport water.

Dahlia

Acacia pycnantha

- National flower of Australia
- Australia's First Peoples used the golden wattle for many purposes ranging from food and medicine to dyes and tools.

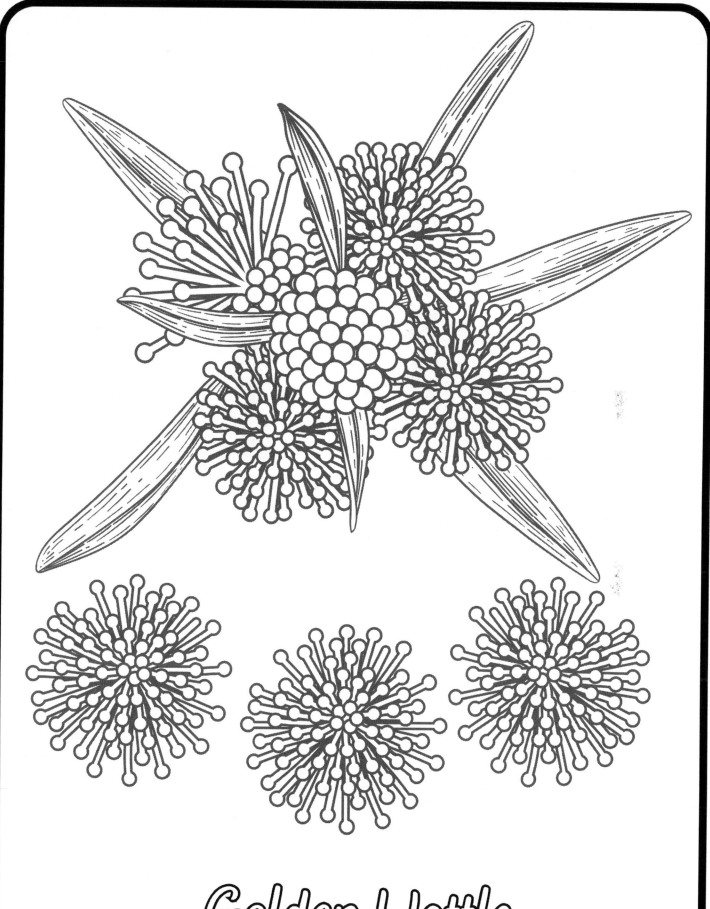

Cantua buxifolia

- National flower of Peru
- Also known as qantu or the Peruvian magic tree, this flower was used in several Incan rituals, as it was believed to keep water pure.

Jasminum sambac

- National flower of the Philippines
- Also known as sampaguita, these are worn in leis, corsages or crowns. Garlands are placed around dignitaries or graduating students.

Jasminum officinale

- National flower of Pakistan
- Also known as chambeli, jasmine is very common in Pakistan. Garlands are usually worn by the bride and groom at weddings.

Chrysanthemum indicum

- National flower of Japan
- Originally brought to Japan from China, chrysanthemums were adopted as the Imperial Seal in the 12th century.

Chrysanthemum

Prunus serrulata

- National flower of Japan (unofficial)
- Also known as sakura, cherry blossoms are one of Japan's most recognizable symbols. The practice of "hanami" means to view flowers and has been practiced since the 8th century.

Prunus mume

- National flower of China
- Plum blossoms bloom in early spring and are used as an offering at Buddhist temples for the Lunar New Year.

Protea cynaroides

- National flower of South Africa
- Protea are some of the oldest flowering plants in the world, with fossil evidence from over 300 million years ago.

King Protea

Gloriosa superba

- National flower of Zimbabwe
- All parts of the plant contain colchicine, which is poisonous. At low doses, it can be used to treat gout or snakebites. At high doses, it is lethal.

Flame Lily

Nelumbo nucifera

- National flower of India
- The lotus flower is associated with several Hindu deities and is a sacred symbol in many religions, serving as a symbol for purity, creation and enlightenment.

Nymphaea

- National flower of Iran
- Water lilies have been symbolic in Iran since ancient times when this flower was a symbol of the goddess of water, Nahid.

Rhododendron arboreum

- National flower of Nepal
- Also known as Lali Gurans, this flower has medicinal uses for patients with dysentery. It can also be pickled and eaten.

Tree Rhododendron

Onopordum acanthium

- National flower of Scotland
- The thistle is featured in many legends, including one from the 13th century where Viking invaders were thwarted by walking barefoot on thistle.

Rosa (many species)

- National flower of USA
- The rose is the national flower of the USA. There are over 20 species of rose that are native to North America, including the Wild Prairie Rose.

Dianthus caryophyllus

- National flower of Spain
- In Spain, flamenco dancers frequently put red carnations in their hair.

Lavandula latifolia

- National flower of Portugal
- Lavender flowers contain oil that acts as both a sedative and a disinfectant. The flowers are also edible.

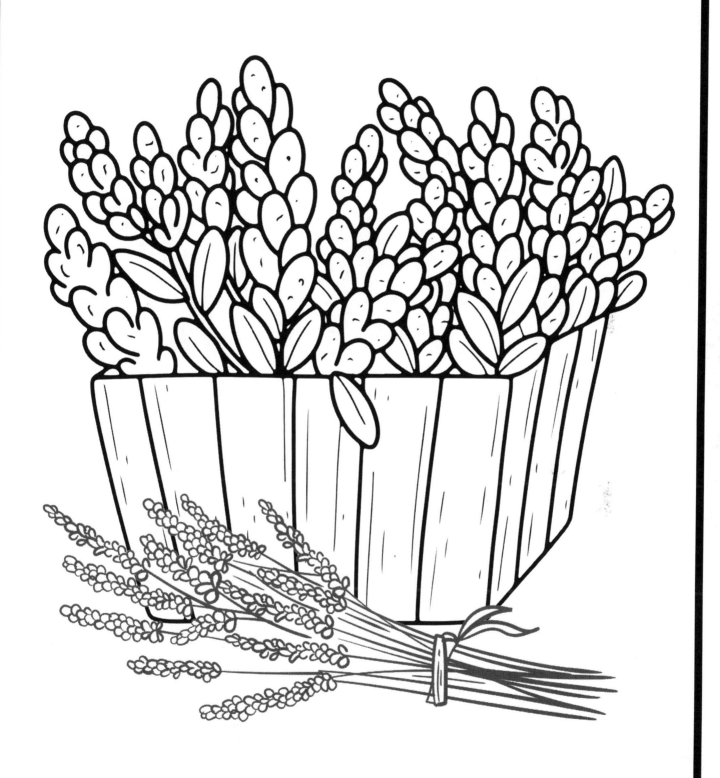

Lavender

Tulipa gesneriana

- National flower of The Netherlands
- Tulips did not originate in The Netherlands, but were brought from Turkey in the 1500's.

Campanula rotundifolia

- National flower of Sweden
- Also known as the bluebell, the harebell became the official national flower of Sweden after winning an historic public vote in 2021.

Harebell

Passiflora caerulea

- National flower of Paraguay
- This flower can be used as tea, as long as care is taken with the leaves, which contain cyanide. However, the cyanide can be boiled away.

Costus spectabilis

- National flower of Nigeria
- The yellow trumpet is a flowering herb with edible flowers that taste fruity, while the roots are used in incense.

Yellow Trumpet

Erythrina crista-galli

- National flower of Argentina
- Sometimes called the cockspur coral, the ceibo tree is a symbol of bravery, which is featured in the legend of Anahi, a Guarani woman.

Paeonia

- National flower of Romania
- Five types of peonies grow wild in Romania, where it has inspired many works of art, music and literature.

Peony

Anemone coronaria

- National flower of the State of Israel
- During the winter, there is a festival known as Darom Adom to celebrate this wildflower.

Sophora

- National flower of New Zealand
- Eight types of kowhai trees are native to New Zealand. The Maori used the flowers as a source of yellow dye.

Hibiscus syriacus

- National flower of South Korea
- The Rose of Sharon is a type of hibiscus that was introduced to the Korean peninsula before the 9th century, where it was used to brew tea.

Rose of Sharon

Hibiscus rosa-sinesis

- National flower of Malaysia
- Also known as rose mallow, this flower can be used as shoe polish. Historically it had many medicinal uses, including for bronchitis.

Bauhinia x blakeana

- National flower of Hong Kong
- The Hong Kong orchid tree is a sterile hybrid, and it is known to have many health benefits. It is featured on Hong Kong's coat of arms.

Zantedeschia aethiopica

- National flower of Ethiopia
- Often associated with weddings, white calla lilies are considered a symbol of peace.

Centaurea cyanus

- National flower of Estonia
- In Estonia, cornflowers typically grow in rye fields, leading to the association of this flower with their staple grain.

Iris croatica

- National flower of Croatia
- In Slavic mythology, irises would appear wherever lightning from the god Perun touched the ground

Calluna vulgaris

- National flower of Norway
- Common purple heather is found all over Norway, where sheep can often be seen grazing this hardy alpine flower.

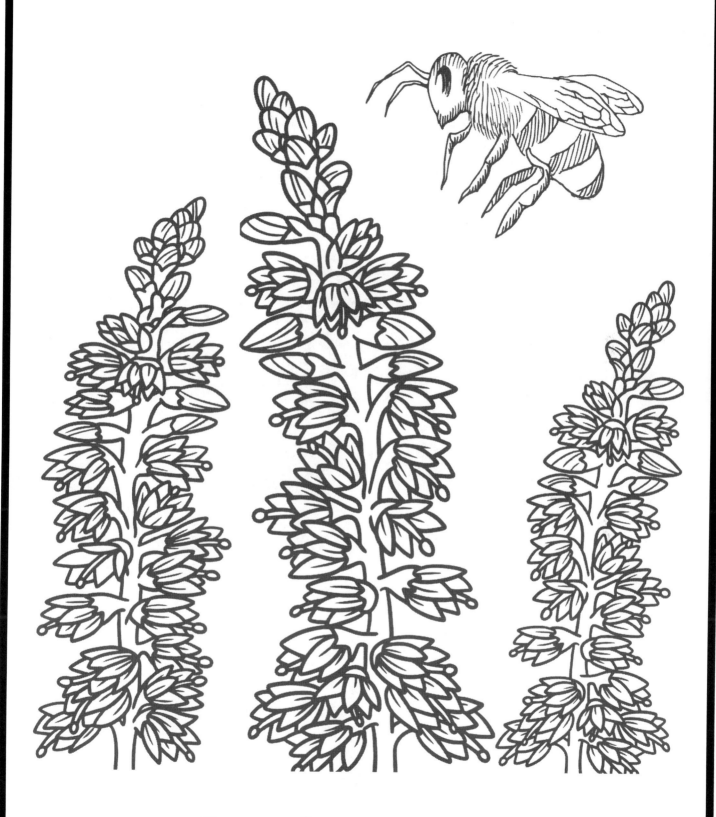

Leontopodium nivale

- National flower of Austria
- Edelweiss has anti-aging properties and is used in cosmetic treatments. Traditionally it was brewed into tea to relieve stomach pain.

Gerbera jamesonii

- National flower of Eritrea
- Gerbera daisies are very common in Eritrea, and are one of the hardiest flowers, able to live for a long time after being cut and put in a vase.

Gerbera Daisy

Matricaria chamomilla

- National flower of Russia
- Frequently used to brew tea, chamomile has been used medicinally for centuries. Chamomile can be found in ancient Russian artwork.

Chamomile

Argyranthemum frutescens

- National flower of Denmark
- Marguerite daisies have been used as a royal symbol and can be seen on coins and medals.

Acanthus mollis

- National flower of Greece
- The shape of the leaf of bear's breeches were used in classic Greek and Roman architechture carved into stonework atop columns.

Nyctaginaceae

- National flower of Grenada
- The colorful bracts or leaves are sometimes mistaken to be the flowers, which are actually the tiny trumpet-shaped flowers inside.

Bougainvillea

Cattleya mossiae

- National flower of Venezuela
- Also known as an "Easter orchid", C. mossiae is native to Venezuela, and is frequently incorporated into religious displays by the Catholic Church.

Cattleya trianae

- National flower of Colombia
- Also known as a "Christmas orchid", C. trianae is endemic to Colombia, where it grows in the cloud forest and blooms in the winter.

Narcissus

- National flower of Wales
- Daffodils bloom around the 1st of March, which is St. David's Day—the feast day of the patron saint of Wales.

Cyclamen libanoticum

- National flower of Lebanon
- This rare flower is native to a small mountainous area. Historically, it has been used in cultural traditions such as weddings.

Cyclamen

Papaver rhoeas

- National flower of Belgium
- The common field poppy, also known as the Flanders poppy, is a symbol of the blood of fallen soldiers during World War I.

Trifolium (either dubium or repens)

- National flower of Ireland
- Shamrocks always have 3 leaves, while clovers can sometimes have 4 leaves. The Celtic druids believed 3 to be a perfect number.

Acer saccharum

- National flower of Canada
- The iconic sugar maple leaf has been a symbol of Canada since at least the 1700s. Maple syrup is an important Canadian resource.

Scientific name of flower

- National flower of COUNTRY
- Interesting fact about the flower

Use this page to test colors and check for bleeding.

Tip: if using markers try putting a blank piece of paper or a piece of plastic underneath each page before coloring.

Note: this page is repeated in the front of the book.

Scientific name of flower

- National flower of COUNTRY
- Interesting fact about the flower

Rainbow Lada Press is an imprint of Rainbow Lada, LLC.

At Rainbow Lada Press, we publish books that bring joy and laughter to people, regardless of who they are.

https://rainbowladapress.com

Interested in more coloring books about flowers or with educational facts? Check out the rest of our coloring books, and a line of beautiful hardback journals!

Thank you for buying this book. I hope it brought a smile to your day!

Janet Hankins